W9-CEM-041

Good

Measures

A Practice Book to Accompany
RULES OF THUMB

Good Measures

A Practice Book to Accompany

RULES OF THUMB

FOURTH EDITION

Jay Silverman

Elaine Hughes

Diana Roberts Wienbroer

Boston, MA   Burr Ridge, IL   Dubuque, IA   Madison, WI
New York, NY   San Francisco, CA   St. Louis, MO
Bangkok   Bogotá   Caracas   Lisbon   London   Madrid   Mexico City
Milan   New Delhi   Seoul   Singapore   Sydney   Taipei   Toronto

GOOD MEASURES: A Practice Book to Accompany *RULES OF THUMB*

Copyright © 2000, 1999 by Jay Silverman, Elaine Hughes, and Diana Roberts Wienbroer. Previous editions © 1994 and 1996. Printed in the United States of America. Except as permitted under the United States Copyright Act of 1976, no part of this publication may be reproduced or distributed in any form or by means, or stored in a data base or retrieval system, without prior written permission of the publisher.

This book is printed on acid-free paper.

1 2 3 4 5 6 7 8 9 0 DOC/DOC 9 0 9 8 7 6 5 4 3 2 1 0 9

ISBN: 0-07-236332-0

Editorial Director: *Phillip A. Butcher*

Senior Sponsoring Editor: *Lisa Moore*

Developmental Editor: *Emily Sparano*

Project Manager: *Christine Parker*

Production Supervisor: *Michael McCormick*

Designers: *Kiera Cunningham* and *Pam Verros*

Compositor: *Shepherd, Inc.*

Typeface: *11/13 Bookman Old Style*

Printer: *R.R. Donnelley & Sons Company*

http://www.mhhe.com/writers

About the Authors

A graduate of Amherst College and the University of Virginia, Jay Silverman has received fellowships from the Fulbright-Hayes Foundation, the Andrew Mellon Foundation, and the National Endowment for the Humanities. Dr. Silverman has taught at Virginia Highlands Community College and at Nassau Community College where he received the Honors Program Award for Excellence in Teaching and where he also teaches in the College Bound Program of the Nassau County Mental Health Association.

Elaine Hughes moved to New York City from Mississippi in 1979 to attend a National Endowment for the Humanities seminar at Columbia University. She has taught writing for more than twenty-five years, primarily at Hinds Community College in Raymond, Mississippi, and at Nassau Community College. Since her retirement from NCC and her return to Mississippi, she has conducted many writing workshops for the Esalen Institute and for other organizations. She is also the author of *Writing from the Inner Self*.

As Chair of the English Department of Nassau Community College for six years, Diana Roberts Wienbroer coordinated a department of 150 faculty members and served on the Executive Council of the Association of Departments of English. Besides teaching writing for over thirty years, both in Texas and New York, she has studied and taught film criticism. She is also the author of *The McGraw-Hill Guide to Electronic Research and Documentation*, 1997.

The authors have also written *Rules of Thumb and Rules of Thumb for Research*, both available from McGraw-Hill.

Contents

PART I: CORRECTNESS

Part II: PUTTING A PAPER TOGETHER

PART III: MEETING SPECIFIC ASSIGNMENTS

PART IV: WRITING WITH ELEGANCE

To the Student

We have written *Good Measures* to give you practice in applying the concepts presented in *Rules of Thumb: A Guide for Writers*. At the top of each page, we've put the corresponding page numbers from *Rules of Thumb* so that you can look up the relevant rule.

Good Measures presents two kinds of exercises. Some are drills that offer a quick way to test your understanding. But drills can take you only so far; the real proof of your knowledge comes in actual writing. Therefore, we've also included writing activities which require you to apply your knowledge. In some cases, the required writing is very brief—making up single sentences. But often we've given longer assignments that we hope will be enjoyable as well as instructive. The drills in *Good Measures* give you ways to "measure" your learning by testing yourself. The writing activities present "measures" you can take to practice new skills and to grow as a writer.

Jay Silverman

Elaine Hughes

Diana Roberts Wienbroer

To the Instructor

We are eager for your reactions to *Good Measures.* We would like to know if it meets your needs in the classroom; we also welcome your suggestions for improvements.

Please send any comments on *Good Measures*—or on *Rules of Thumb*—to us directly:

Jay Silverman, Elaine Hughes, Diana Roberts Wienbroer
Department of English
Nassau Community College
Garden City, New York 11530-6793

Acknowledgments

We particularly wish to thank two people for their enthusiasm and support for *Good Measures:* Beverly Jensen, whose encouragement and ideas contributed to every page; and Laurie PiSierra, whose expert editor's eye guided the quality of the book.

Special thanks go to our colleagues—Jeanne Hunter and Hedda Marcus, at Nassau Community College, and Susan Finlayson, at Adirondack Community College, who gave us sound advice on content and audience.

We are also grateful for careful reviews, accompanied by specific suggestions for improvements by Robin Calitri, Merced College; Bill Nagle, Middlesex Community College; and Nell Ann Pickett, Hinds Community College.

Our thanks also go to John Fitzgibbon, Jane Malmo, and Ernest Migliaccio for their creative ideas; to Kiera Cunningham for her inviting design; and to Lesley Denton, Alison Husting, and Tim Julet at McGraw-Hill for their consistent support of the project.

We are especially grateful to our students who provided responses to the exercises and helped us to shape the book, and in particular to Jennifer Franceschi-Wood for permission to reprint her research paper.

Jay Silverman

Elaine Hughes

Diana Roberts Wienbroer

P A R T   I

Correctness

Confusing Words

AFFECT / EFFECT, ITS / IT'S

In the following sentences, cross out any incorrect words and write corrections above them.

Example: The trade deficit continues to ~~effect~~ *affect* the economy.

Affect / Effect

1. The special affects made the whole production magical.

2. A hot toddy can affect how you feel when you have a bad cold.

3. After an MRI (magnetic resonance imaging), the magnets have no lasting effect on the patient.

4. The tall man in the second row effected the view of the entire audience.

5. A household fire effects the whole family, and the effects last for years.

Its / It's

1. Even if its July, its still best to pack a sweater for a trip to Maine.

2. Ingrid Bergman had only a minute to return the key to it's proper place before the villain would notice its absence.

3. The snake vibrates it's rattle when it senses that it's in danger.

4. Its a miracle that no one was hurt when the car rolled over on it's side.

5. When its noon in New York, its six o'clock in Paris.

LAY / LIE, PASSED / PAST

In the following sentences, cross out any incorrect words and write corrections above them.

Example: The clue to the corpse's identity was l̶a̶y̶i̶n̶g̶ *lying* in the bushes.

Lay / Lie

1. Cleopatra laid on the divan, eating grapes; as she got up, she laid the grape stems on the cushion.

2. Once the foundation was in place, they began laying the floors, but the manager continued lying about the date of occupancy.

3. Every night while I was laying in bed trying to sleep, the smell from the paper factory kept me awake.

4. The archivist laid each picture flat in the drawer, but the last one was laying off-center.

5. The patient lay comatose while the nurses quickly prepared the instruments for surgery.

Passed / Past

1. The train sped passed the platform of waiting passengers.

2. The cat has never eaten tuna in the past because we had always bought the kind that was packed in oil.

3. Kip past the ball behind his back to set up Nancy, who made a slam dunk.

4. Several years ago, the total of the human population past five billion.

5. In crossbreeding tulips, growers hope that the most attractive traits from the past can be genetically past on.

THAN / THEN, THEIR / THERE / THEY'RE

In the following sentences, cross out any incorrect words and write corrections above them.

then
Example: Chop all the ingredients; ~~than~~ heat the wok.

Than / Then

1. Beethoven's late quartets are more extraordinary then his earlier, more popular music.

2. Advertisements urge you to buy whatever you want and then pay later.

3. The shares in L.A.Gear are worth 25 percent less today then they were last week.

4. In the dry season, this canal clogs up now and than, diminishing the water supply.

5. The chiefs in the southern part of Cameroon exercise much less power then the chiefs in the west.

Their / There / They're

1. Every year in August, their is a Twins Day Festival in Twinsburg, Ohio.

2. In *The Brothers Karamazov*, all of the brothers resent there father's silliness.

3. We turned the corner and there were my aunt and uncle standing in the middle of the dusty road next to there stalled car.

4. When overtime work is available, their always the ones who show up first.

5. There the only people I know who would rather read about a place than go there.

TO / TOO / TWO, YOUR / YOU'RE

In the following sentences, cross out any incorrect words and write corrections above them.

to

Example: Employers are required by law t̶o̶o̶ scrutinize the investments included in pension plans.

To / Too / Two

1. In order to snorkel safely, you need to have the proper

   equipment.

2. To many is as bad as to few.

3. Malcolm's hair is to thin to wear combed over the top of his head.

4. Evidence has recently come to light that to much passive smoke

   is harmful to one's health.

5. Whitman's subject matter was to risqué, for many readers of his

   day—and ours to.

Your / You're

1. Your lucky that you've never been in Uncle Eddie's fish store on a

   hot day.

2. When your cue comes, act as if your not sure which way to walk.

3. You're first step is to wash your hands with an antibacterial

   solution.

4. When your in a foreign country, your sense of time is altered.

5. You're going to be surprised when you start to record you're sugar

   consumption—one cup of catsup may contain seventeen

   teaspoons of sugar.

A / AN, ACCEPT / EXCEPT, ETC., GOOD / WELL, LOOSE / LOSE, KNEW / KNOW / NEW / NO / NOW, HAVE / OF, QUIET / QUIT / QUITE, WERE / WE'RE / WHERE, WEATHER / WHETHER, WHO'S / WHOSE, WOMAN / WOMEN

In the following sentences, cross out any incorrect words and write corrections above them.

women

Example: I don't believe that any ~~woman~~ were interviewed for the position of comptroller.

1. A room full of three-year-olds will never be quite.

2. Ara decided to except the director's criticism except for the comment about her favorite yellow hat.

3. After a night of driving through the jungle, the jeep had three lose wheels and the driver didn't even now it.

4. If the weather is favorable, were climbing to the top of Arthur's Seat when we return to Edinburgh.

5. During a play, the performers know who's going to enter next, based on whose cue has been spoken.

6. Trevor would have accepted the duchess's invitation, accept that he had already decided to elope that night.

7. Sally Ride, the first women in space, has since served as a presidential adviser on scientific research.

8. It was never a question of whether he would be a doctor, but weather he would be an orthopedist or a pediatrician.

9. Costello thought that Abbott was asking "Whose on first?" when Abbott was actually telling him about a first baseman named Who.

10. In the desert, were the temperatures rise and drop suddenly, you would have to wear extra layers of clothing.

11. The trucker has to drive quiet a long way before he is able to quite for the night.

12. The uncontrolled forest fire might of destroyed their house, their garage, their car, etc.

13. There has been much discussion of late as to whether a women will be chosen as the next ambassador.

14. In typical scenes from Chekhov, the characters know that now is the time to speak their true feelings or they will forever loose their chance—yet they say nothing.

15. During World War II, the military would not except a African American serving in the same unit as white Americans.

16. They should of known that there would be problems bringing so much luggage onto the plane.

17. The loose rock debris, called "scree," makes it very easy to loose one's footing.

18. Loons are quiet good swimmers and fliers, but they cannot walk very good.

19. Because of the knew code strip in one-hundred-dollar bills, it's harder know to pass counterfeit bills than it used to be.

20. The doughnut was originally called "dow-knot," a English treat made each year for Christmas.

CUMULATIVE EXERCISE

In the following paragraph, cross out any incorrect words and write corrections above them. For example, the first line should be corrected to read:

too
Many readers find the last part of *Huckleberry Finn* to be ~~to~~ drawn out.

Many readers find the last part of *Huckleberry Finn* to be to drawn

out. There disappointed by the way Tom Sawyer dominates Huck.

They're also uncomfortable when Tom makes Jim, the runaway

slave, go through childish games in order to win the freedom he

should of had in the first place. While Jim is laying chained up in a   5

tiny cabin, Tom makes an elaborate but needless plan of escape.

The plan seems to take forever. Once readers have past the

excitement of Tom's arrival, the book looses its charm. And yet,

their disappointment doesn't ruin their experience of the novel. Its

far less important to them then the joyful effect of most of the   10

book.

CUMULATIVE EXERCISE

In the following paragraph, cross out any incorrect words and write corrections above them. For example, the first line should be corrected to read:

You're

The serviceman casually told Ilene, "~~Your~~ going to have to buy a

The serviceman casually told Ilene, "Your going to have to buy a

new hard drive for this computer. Your present one is too dirty."

This was not good news. His statement effected Ilene in several

ways: her mouth got to dry to speak; she felt the need to lay down;

and the room dimmed so that she couldn't see very good. She   5

thought to herself, "Where are we going to find the money to pay

for this? We're a nonprofit organization. Its going to cost us a lot of

money. The expiration date on the warranty has now past. Or has

it?" Their was a glimmer of hope. She remembered something.

"They're not going to like this, but it was their idea in the first   10

place." Ilene searched through her desk for the service contract.

She found it, and there, on the bottom line, was the following

sentence: "If you purchase this machine in the month of February,

then you receive two additional months of free service." This was more then she could have hoped for. They had purchased the   15

machine last February 29th—the Leap Year Special. Ilene

congratulated herself for being one smart women!

Writing Activity

Select any word from column A, and use it in a sentence about any topic in column B. Be sure to use all the words and all the topics.

For example, if you choose *there* and *something that leaks,* you might write

There is nothing as maddening as a dripping faucet at midnight.

Column A	Column B
you're	something that tickles
its	something that is clogged
too	something that leaks
than	something that smells wonderful
there	something that stinks
affect	something that burns
their	something that turns over

One Word or Two?

In the following paragraphs, look for two words where there should be one, or one word where there should be two. Cross out any incorrect words and write the correct words above them. For example, the first line should be corrected to read:

Anyone
~~Any one~~ who has ever seen an exhibit of early American quilts can

Any one who has ever seen an exhibit of early American quilts can

understand why quilts, nowadays, are being recognized as an

important form of American art. Some how the women of early

America—for it was the women who made quilts—perfected the

chore into an art form. During the years when the United States   5

was first being settled, everybody made quilts out of necessity. In

fact, they were an early form of recycling. Worn clothing was torn a

part and cut into alot of different-sized pieces. These scraps were

then sewn together randomly to make covers and backs. Quilts

made this way were called "crazy" quilts. Sometimes they were   10

stuffed with straw, sometimes with corn husks. Through out the

harsh winters the quilts helped to keep the settlers warm.

In fact, the haphazard piecing of odd scraps was only the

beginning. Inspiteof the crude materials that the women often had

to work with, the cutting and piecing of the scraps of fabric   15

became increasingly intricate. Nevertheless, with out the benefit of

sewing machines these women created beautiful hand-sewn quilts

in order to help both themselves and eachother. Nobody could

deny that the quilts are works of art.

Spelling

EI / IE

Insert either *ei* or *ie* into the spaces in the words below.

Example: n___ghbor   n*ei*ghbor

1. dec____ve

2. bel____ve

3. fr____nd

4. fr____ght

5. p___ce

6. n___ce

7. c___ling

8. s___ze

9. anc____nt

10. w___rd

11. br____f

12. th____r

13. rec____ve

14. v____n

15. l___sure

16. w____gh

17. conc____ted

18. rec____pt

19. for____gn

20. sl____gh

Spelling

T OR TT? P OR PP?

In each of the words below, fill in the blank with one or two of the letter indicated.

Example: dro___ing   dro*pp*ing

1. wri____er	(t)	11. dra____ed	(g)
2. occa____ion	(s)	12. cra____ed	(m)
3. begi____ing	(n)	13. hi____ing	(d)
4. sto____ed	(p)	14. ru____ing	(l)
5. occu____ed	(r)	15. sho____ed	(p)
6. whi____ed	(p)	16. bla____ing	(m)
7. wi____ed	(p)	17. hi____ing	(t)
8. jo____ing	(g)	18. wri____en	(t)
9. qui____ing	(t)	19. dro____ing	(p)
10. refe____ed	(r)	20. ro____ery	(b)

Spelling

WORD ENDINGS

In the following paragraph, cross out any incorrect words and write corrections above them. For example, the first line should be corrected to read:

Coming
~~Comming~~ home with a new baby can be a trying time as well as a

Comming home with a new baby can be a trying time as well as a

joyous one. In the begining parents may not be prepared for the

intensity of the baby's crying. Psychologist confirm that crying

causes much frustration in new families. The baby's cries can have

many meanings: "I need food"; "I need to be held"; "I need to be   5

changed." But when feeding, holding, and changing don't work,

parents don't know what they are suppose to do, and they feel like

crying themselves. Gradually, however, the parents learn to

interpret different cries; gradually they learn tricks for relieving

discomforts (like walking or dancing while holding the baby close)   10

and thus stoping the cries; and gradualy the baby becomes more

use to the inner and outer discomforts of daily life. The biggest

danger for familys at these times is that frustration might spill over into fighting between parents or into child abuse. New parents

need to know that their frustration is normal and that within three   15

months things will be better. Instead of takeing their anger out on

each other or on the baby, they should help each other through the

trying times. Latter they may look back with pride, fondness, and

even humor at the adventure of their first three months of

parenthood.

Spelling

PREFIXES AND SUFFIXES

In the lists below, underline the misspelled word and write the correct spelling in the space to the right. (Only one word in each line is misspelled.)

Example: postscript pastime <u>partime</u> halftime   *part-time*

1. disappear disatisfaction disappoint disillusion   _____

2. unsatisfactory uninterested unecessary unnoticed

   _____

3. hopful careful really lonely   _____

4. environment government committment disappointment

   _____

5. totally truely hopefully finally   _____

6. debatable incredible sensable noticeable   _____

7. arguement appointment suddenness carefulness

   _____

8. fourty ninety fourth nineteenth   _____

9. caring arguing loving debateing   _____

10. tarring dragging gunning begining   _____

12. drugged dragged dropped interferred _____

13. believe conceited receive piece _____

14. truly really succesfully lonely _____

15. hopeful noticeable ninty careful _____

16. dissatisfaction unnoticed dissappointment misspell

_____

17. embarrass necessary usually occasion _____

18. writer quitting writting quitter _____

19. restlessness thinness occurence openness _____

20. definitely seperate criticism ridiculous _____

Spelling

CUMULATIVE EXERCISE

In the following paragraphs, cross out any incorrect words and write corrections above them. For example, the first line should be corrected to read:

definitely
Earning a Ph.D. is ~~definately~~ a demanding process. Often the

Earning a Ph.D. is definately a demanding process. Often the

graduate school catalog suggests that candidates can recieve their

degrees after four years of work, but usally at least five years are

necessary.

The process consist of three stages. In the begining, the students   5

do two years of course work. Then they take several months

studing for the preliminary exam. This exam usually combines a

written and an oral test. Finally, the students begin writting their

dissertations. A dissertation presents an original opinion about a

specialized topic of intrest. The students aren't totaly finished until   10

they defend their dissertations in front of a panel of professors.

The Ph.D. candidates are suppose to do all of this while also trying to make enough money to live on. Fellowships are not as generous as they use to be; candidates must teach and work parttime while preparing for their degrees. Nevertheless, the intellectual 15 excitement of the work, the satisfaction of acheiving the doctorate, and the possibility of becoming a college professor drive many students to complete the long process.

Capitalization

In the following sentences, add any necessary capitalization. For example, examine the following sentence:

> my english professor, dr. fogarty, gave up the medical profession to become a college teacher.

This sentence should be corrected to read:

> My English professor, Dr. Fogarty, gave up the medical profession to become a college teacher.

1. the inauguration of general washington as the first president took place in new york, the nation's original capital.

2. my friend albert is from deadsville, nevada, and doesn't know a chevrolet from a jeep.

3. our good neighbors, mr. and mrs. chaney, gave us their old set of encyclopaedia brittanica.

4. the first coca cola was bottled in vicksburg, mississippi, a small southern town, in 1894, by the biedenhorn family.

5. if you run a red light and cause a wreck, you may end up needing a doctor as well as a lawyer.

6. when marylynne graduated from high school last spring, her grandfather gave her his old cadillac.

7. on wednesday we saw a production of cat on a hot tin roof at the williamstown theater.

8. the reading list for professor schneider's american history 201 is two pages long.

9. last week we went to yankee stadium and saw the yankees beat the kansas city royals with a wild ninth-inning rally.

10. before caryl chessman was executed, he led a crusade to persuade the governor and legislature of california to abolish capital punishment.

Abbreviations and Numbers

In the following paragraph, cross out any incorrect words and write corrections above them. For example, the first line should be corrected to read:

brothers
The Grimm ~~bros.~~ probably never expected that they would be best

The Grimm bros. probably never expected that they would be best

known for the 210 German fairy tales that they collected and

published in the yrs. between 1812 and 1850. Collecting fairy tales

was only one project undertaken by these 2 bros. They were

involved w/ all aspects of German cultural history. They collected   5

myths, legends, and medieval lit. They began an extensive

dictionary tracing the history of German words (similar to our *OED,*

the Oxford English Dictionary). Jacob Grimm discovered the links

between the Germanic languages of northern Europe (such as

Eng.) & the Romance languages of southern Europe (such as   10

Spanish and Italian). The Grimm bros. were also politically involved

and were in a group of 7 profs. who lost their jobs for disagreeing

with the govt.

Writing Activity

Write directions for getting from school to your house. Write in terms of the mode of transportation that you normally take— for example, walking, driving, cycling, or taking the bus. Use numbers and abbreviations correctly. For example, you might write:

> Corlears School is located at 324 West 15th Street next to El Cid Restaurant. When you leave the front door, turn right and walk to the corner of Eighth Avenue. . . .

Apostrophes

In the following sentences, add an apostrophe wherever necessary. For example, examine the following sentence:

No one sees her, but the narrators voice dominates the opening scene.

This sentence should be corrected to read:

No one sees her, but the narrator's voice dominates the opening scene.

1. The compositor says its not fair that he gets paid so little

   compared to the editor.

2. The new banks real estate holdings arent worth as much as the

   investors think.

3. In the summer, Larry spends his days exploring Mr. Ottomanellis

   meadow.

4. Depending on its half-life, a radioactive isotope can be dangerous

   for only a few seconds or for years.

5. A good nights sleep has its own quiet pleasures.

6. An article in todays newspaper reported that the president doesnt

   know of any improprieties on the part of the attorney general.

7. E.T. eats Reeses Pieces, not M&Ms.

8. "Odd, isnt it?" asks Fred. "Everyones dead and Ruths a

   millionaire."

9. When youve chopped all the ingredients, youre ready to start

   cooking Uncle Lens stir-fried shrimp.

10. Paulette doesnt put up with her managers rudeness.

Apostrophes

In the following paragraphs, add an apostrophe wherever necessary. For example, the first sentence should be corrected to read:

Ira's house is a world of its own.

Iras house is a world of its own. Downstairs lives his Uncle Abe. Ira never enters Abes apartment. Upstairs, in the front room, Iras parents sit for hours and talk. Pete, the old beagle, sprawls on a hooked rug. In the back room, the boys play ping pong. Iras ping pong table takes up the entire room, leaving a space of less than eighteen inches for each of the players. 5

Beverly sits on her mothers porch and shells peas. The plunk, plunk, plunk of the peas landing in the round tin tray blends in with the raindrops drumming on the screens. Its Fourth of July and there will be salmon and peas for breakfast. The rains untimely burst wont affect her day. Shes sure that it will pass over in time for this afternoons party and this evenings picnic. 5

35

Writing Activity

Write a paragraph about a house or apartment that you remember from childhood. Write in the present tense, as if you were there right now. Be sure to use some words that need apostrophes. Here is an example of how you might begin:

Every morning at Aunt Lillie's house on Farmer Street, Uncle Tabo cooks a big breakfast. We children can't wait to drink Uncle Tabo's big mugs of coffee milk. . . .

Write a paragraph about a teacher— past or present— and his or her character, quirks, methods, clothes, etc. Be sure to use some words that need apostrophes. Here is an example of how you might begin:

I couldn't believe Mr. Small's love of math. He enjoyed writing examples on the board filled with x's and y's and impossible numbers. . . .

Consistent Pronouns

Correct each sentence to make the nouns, pronouns, and their verbs consistent. For example, look at the following sentence:

A great chef doesn't need to measure their ingredients.

There are several ways to correct this sentence:

A great chef doesn't need to measure the ingredients.

Great chefs don't need to measure their ingredients.

A great chef doesn't need to measure his or her ingredients.

1. If someone is disrupting the performance, they should be asked to leave.

2. A person should be careful not to break the yolk when you separate the egg.

3. To be a good waiter, one must be able to stay on their feet and smile for hours.

4. Even on cloudy days, when you may not seem to be exposed to sunlight, one should take precautions against ultraviolet rays.

5. When I wear unusual clothes, people look at you in a strange way.

6. A wise politician will be judicious with their promises.

7. When someone meets someone for the first time, they should try to remember his or her name.

8. I got mad; it does make you upset when people don't listen.

9. If an opera student is serious about their voice, they know the importance of breath control and they relax before a performance.

10. A person who is traveling should know not to schedule their vacation timetables too tightly.

Correct Pronouns

Correct the pronouns in the following sentences where necessary. In some cases, you may need to change the word order.

My mother and I

Example: ~~Me and my mother~~ would head out to school each day with me crying my eyes out.

1. He and his sister hope to practice law with my father and I.

2. For Amelia and I, both language majors, the year to study abroad was our chief consideration in choosing the college.

3. That controversy is for the Office of Consumers Affairs and her to resolve.

4. We sued her lawyer and her.

5. Oscar Hammerstein II may be our country's most influential lyricist; Richard Rodgers and him wrote America's most popular musical comedies.

6. Anna Karenina was torn between he and her husband.

7. Butch Cassidy and him robbed banks, from the American West to Bolivia.

8. For years, the Russians were our enemies, yet in our histories there are great similarities between them and us.

9. Between you and I, the jazz pianist should have won the competition.

10. The new insurance policy will require a smaller deductible for my husband and myself.

11. Frances and myself had the dirty job of cleaning all the shower curtains before she and I could pick up our paychecks.

12. Carl makes better cheesecake than me.

13. Carl works in the kitchen better with Margaret than with me.

14. Carl works in the kitchen better with Margaret than I do.

15. My sister is a better carpenter than me, but I play the guitar better than her.

16. Cleopatra loved Julius Caesar, but she loved Marc Antony even more than him.

17. Caesar conquered a great territory, but Napoleon conquered even

    more than him.

18. Guess whom is coming for dinner.

19. Whom should I say is calling?

20. We bought tickets for he and she for *The King and I.*

Writing Activity

Write a sentence using each of these pairs of pronouns correctly:

Example: Both Felicia and I like to swim in the lake at night.

1. Felicia and I

2. Mel and her

3. them and me

4. him and her

5. Lori and me

6. The committee and he

7. my friend and I

8. she and Benny

9. the players and him

10. my cousins and me

Vague Pronouns

Revise these sentences so that none of the pronouns is vague. For example, look at the following sentences:

Tim ordered Chinese food for us instead of pizza. This is my favorite take-out food.

There are two ways to interpret "this" in the sentence, and therefore two possible revisions:

Pizza is my favorite take-out food.
or
Chinese food is my favorite.

A better option is to combine sentences:

Tim ordered my favorite take-out food—Chinese—instead of pizza.

1. Use a mildly abrasive cleanser in which the tub enamel will be

    protected.

2. Food advertising rarely emphasizes vegetables, which is terrible

    for public health.

3. Ernie never eats raw peppers, mussels, or mustard. It makes him

    break out.

4. Over 75 percent of the inmates in New York State's prisons come

    from just seven neighborhoods in New York City, which has

    community leaders searching for solutions.

6. Every June, honeysuckle floods the roads of Virginia with perfume.

7. The twins placed an ad in the paper: "Last Day to Send in Your Dollar!"—and over a thousand people did.

8. I shut off the alarm clock and rolled onto my back.

9. There has never been a simple method for figuring federal income tax.

10. In the Battle of Gettysburg, over five thousand horses were killed.

11. Eddie Sauter, who is a major jazz arranger, recently did the arrangements for Stan Getz's album, *Focus*.

12. The cemetery flowers are either plastic or wilted.

13. That's the reason no one wants to lend her money anymore.

14. Lift the tab and pull back to remove the foil covering before inserting the cartridge into the printer cradle.

15. Introducing the dean, Marylin reversed his first and last names.

16. A number of mysteries incorporate recipes into their plots; Rex Stout's *Too Many Cooks* is one of the best.

17. Clean the upholstery regularly with a commercial leather cream, saddle soap, or a mild solution of vinegar and water.

18. In her paintings, Georgia O'Keefe gave sensuousness to flowers and bones.

19. Jane and Norman hired the catering service and engaged two bands for the wedding reception.

20. "Dumpster Diving" is the term for salvaging usable items from other people's trash; however, this practice is against the law because whatever is put out as garbage is the property of the Sanitation Department.

Recognizing Complete Sentences

WRITING ACTIVITY

Write two sentences in each of the following patterns. For example, you might write:

Simple Sentence:
The Queen Anne cherries were rotten.
There you go again.

Simple Sentence with introductory phrase:
In the morning, the clouds still hung low over the fields.
On our back porch stood the old refrigerator.

1. Simple sentence

2. Simple sentence with introductory phrase

3. Simple sentence with two subjects and one verb

4. Simple sentence with one subject and two verbs

5. Compound sentence connected with *and* or *but*

6. Compound sentence connected with *however*

7. Complex sentence using *when* or *after*

8. Complex sentence beginning with *If* or *Because*

9. Complex sentence using *if* or *because* in the middle

10. Compound-complex sentence

Sentence Fragments

In the exercises below, correct any fragments by attaching them to a sentence or by changing the wording. For example, examine the following:

Madame Bovary abandons her husband and little daughter. In order to experience life to its fullest.

Here are some possible corrections:

Madame Bovary abandons her husband and little daughter in order to experience life to its fullest.
or
Madame Bovary abandons her husband and little daughter. She wants to experience life to its fullest.
or
In order to experience life to its fullest, Madame Bovary abandons her husband and little daughter.

1. There are several subtypes of detective fiction. One being the hard-boiled school.

2. The prompter stands just backstage with the script. Whispering everybody's cues.

3. When he returned years later to help his mother move. He dug for the box exactly where he had buried it.

4. Swimming techniques vary depending on the choppiness of the water. Swimming in the ocean, for example, is different from other kinds of swimming.

5. The record sales figure for avocados each year is for the week of the Super Bowl. Presumably for all the guacamole dip—estimated at 6,000 tons.

6. The financial planner advised them to make a realistic budget. To figure out where their cash was going, then begin saving or investing in a mutual fund.

7. Gregor Mendel discovered the patterns of genetics. By observing how peas grow and reproduce.

8. In his later years, Matisse cut colored paper into ornate collages. Because he could no longer handle a paintbrush.

9. Einstein didn't clutter his mind with "useless" numbers. Such as his home telephone number.

10. I thought that Fred was dependable. That he would be at the restaurant at closing time to pick me up.

Sentence Fragments

The following paragraph contains sentence fragments. Correct them by changing either punctuation or wording. For example, the first line can be corrected to read:

The divorce rate was relatively low up until the 1950s.
or
Up until the 1950s, the divorce rate was relatively low.

The divorce rate was relatively low. Up until the 1950s. Then in the

1970s, it began to skyrocket. Many factors contributed to this:

People beginning to think more about individual fulfillment.

Religious restraints becoming looser. Women gaining a new

capacity to be economically independent. The divorce rate has   5

grown so much in the past two decades that each year for every

two marriages there is one divorce. Today it is not unusual for

children to see their parents divorce. Then see one or both of their

parents remarry and maybe even divorce again. Statistics say little

about the painful and frightening experience that children go   10

through. Especially the adolescents in the family. Many

adjustments follow: Living in a household with only one parent, a

loss in economic and social status, and sometimes a change of

residence. Coping with a divorce in the family is best done through

counseling and support groups. To assure that history will not   15

necessarily repeat itself in the future.

Run-on Sentences

Correct any run-on sentences by changing either punctuation or wording. For example, the first sentence can be corrected to read:

Tradition had it that the ghost appeared always on July 7th. It appeared only to someone who was not a member of the immediate family.

Note: You can also use a semicolon after *July 7th* instead of a period.

Tradition had it that the ghost appeared always on July 7th, it

appeared only to someone who was not a member of the

immediate family. On July 7, 1967, Dr. Rolph Dumaine was visiting

the Beverleys, he was sitting on the back porch. Ann Beverley

served him his second mint julep; she began to describe the death   5

of her favorite dog Jeb Stuart. Suddenly Dr. Dumaine turned to her

and asked, in a voice mildly curious, "Who is the woman with the

long red hair, I haven't been introduced to her?" Ann Beverley's

face lost all its expression. It was as blank as a March day's sky.

"Red-haired, you say? What was she wearing?" "A yellow dress   10

with a wide green belt, she was heading toward the library." Ann

Beverley fainted, the old dog began to howl. Dr. Dumaine felt a

cold sweat trickle down his neck. "It's July 7th," he said to himself.

"Why do I feel cold?"

Run-on Sentences

Correct any run-on sentences in the exercises below by adding punctuation or by changing the wording where necessary. For example, look at the following sentence:

Mozart deserved a better end, he died penniless and was buried in an unmarked grave.

Here are three possible corrections:

Mozart deserved a better end. He died penniless and was buried in an unmarked grave.
or
Mozart deserved a better end; however, he died penniless and was buried in an unmarked grave.
or
Mozart, who deserved a better end, died penniless and was buried in an unmarked grave.

1. The male emperor penguin holds the egg on top of his feet, he does this for two months at a time.

2. There is a secret to cooking good hard-boiled eggs, they should never be boiled.

3. A kitten can sleep in one spot for hours, other times it prowls, stalks, pounces on imaginary prey.

4. An inexpensive styrofoam cooler saved their lives, they clung to it for hours after their boat capsized.

6. Most children are natural artists therefore they should be encouraged to draw and paint.

7. Most children are natural artists but they often quit drawing when they grow up.

8. Since most children are natural artists they should be encouraged to draw and paint.

9. Most children are natural artists they should be encouraged to draw and paint.

10. Children should be encouraged to draw and paint. Since most of them are natural artists.

Sentence Fragments and Run-on Sentences

Continue these sentences and then add any necessary punctuation. You may need to change capitalization, but do not change the original wording. For example, if the exercise sentence reads

I went to the zoo although

you might write

I went to the zoo although I had only an hour.
or
I went to the zoo. Although I had only an hour, I saw all the birds.

1. I went to the zoo however

2. I went to the zoo but

3. I went to the zoo it's

4. I went to the zoo then

5. I went to the zoo especially

6. I try to avoid fatty foods therefore

7. I try to avoid fatty foods which

8. I try to avoid fatty foods nevertheless

9. I try to avoid fatty foods such as

10. I try to avoid fatty foods if

Sentence Fragments and Run-on Sentences

Correct any sentence fragments or run-on sentences by changing punctuation or wording. For example, the first sentence can be corrected several ways:

> Some people can never pass a pinball machine without stopping to play a game. They get hooked on the challenge of keeping the ball on the move.

(Note: You can also use a semicolon after "game" instead of a period.)

> *or*
> Some people can never pass a pinball machine without stopping to play a game because they get hooked on the challenge of keeping the ball on the move.

Some people can never pass a pinball machine without stopping to

play a game they get hooked on the challenge of keeping the ball

on the move. And racking up a score of a million points or more.

The builders of these machines are smart; they add pops and

whirrs, blinking lights, music, and sometimes even an alluring   5

voice. Which calls out to you to come and play a game. If you give

in to the temptation and insert a quarter into the slot. A round

metallic ball will come up on the right side of the machine. Then

the game starts. You pull a plunger-like instrument back. This sets

the ball in motion. It scoots around the surface doing many things   10

59

magazine around the world. His photographs are bold and

straightforward, he projects a cool, clean, thoroughly modern

image. His style has changed with the times over the years. That is

why he is still considered one of the best fashion photographers of

the day. And a legend in his own right. 15

Writing Activities

Write a description of a place that you love to visit. Tell what you love about being there. Check your description carefully for sentence fragments and run-on sentences. Here is an example of how you might begin:

> In the fall I hike down the Natchez Trace to lie on the haystacks that farmers leave in the fields. Lounging up on top, reading a book, drinking Coca-Cola, and muching parched peanuts, I feel like I'm in heaven. . . .

Write a paragraph telling about the most dramatic weather you've ever been in. Use each of these words or phrases at least once:

however   it   for example   therefore   they

Then go back and check your punctuation carefully for sentence fragments and run-on sentences. Here is an example of how you might begin:

> As soon as we heard the flood warnings, we left the square dance; however, we didn't leave soon enough. It was raining so hard that the windshield washers couldn't keep pace, so Pat had to lean out the car window to see. . . .

Word Endings

-ED

Read the following paragraphs and correct any errors in word endings by adding or deleting *-d* or *-ed*. In some cases you may need to change the spelling of the verb. For example, the first sentence should be corrected to read:

qualified
Last summer, Glenda ~~qualify~~ to serve as a grand juror.

Last summer, Glenda qualify to serve as a grand juror. She and twenty-two others had to decided whether suspects should be tried. Usually, the prosecutor presented two witnesses. The first, the victim of the crime, would tell what happen. This witness could tell only what he or she actually saw and heard. In many cases, the victim actually chased the suspect while calling for help. The second witness was usually the police officer who made the arrest. Both witnesses would testified that the victim saw the suspect in the officer's custody. Normally, this evidence was enough to justify a trial.

But sometimes the suspect himself or herself did testify. The suspect usually claimed to have just been passing by when the police suddenly make the arrest. These cases were harder to

decide. The jurors didn't want to bring an innocent person to trial.

Usually, however, the suspect blundered into contradicting his or

her testimony or lying in an obvious way. When the story didn't

make sense, or when the suspect had been seen by two eye-

witnesses, the jurors had less of a problem. After much discussion,

these suspects, too, were usually sent to trial.

Tangled Sentences

DANGLERS

Revise these sentences to correct the danglers. For example, look at the following sentence:

Smelling powerfully of fish, I walked past the seafood market.

This sentence can be corrected to read:

I walked past the seafood market, which smelled powerfully of fish.

1. Last seen wandering vaguely, the police couldn't find Alex's uncle.

2. Rolled into the operating room on a stretcher, the doctor

   prepared to remove my appendix.

3. Pat was thrilled to finally get a bite but, reeling up the line too

   fast, the trout got away.

4. A colossal catastrophe, the firemen arrived at the burning

   chemistry lab.

5. Hanging from the chandelier, the astonished diners looked up at

   Mark's boots.

6. Walking across the soft spring soil, worm holes dimpled the surface.

7. Glowering at each other from opposite corners, the crowd grew tense waiting for the two wrestlers to meet in the middle of the ring.

8. A famous actor, the audience was nevertheless bored by Edward Kean's performance that night.

9. A meticulous planner, the suspense films of Alfred Hitchcock were designed so thoroughly that he did not even need to see the finished film to know what it looked like.

10. To practice medicine, not only a medical degree but internship and residency are required.

Tangled Sentences

MIXED SENTENCE PATTERNS

Revise these sentences to correct the mixed sentence patterns. For example, look at the following sentence:

In history has shown that people who speak out can change the world.

Here are two ways that this sentence can be revised:

History has shown that people who speak out can change the world.
or
In history we learn that people who speak out can change the world.

1. If one of the train engineers has been taking drugs could cause a fatal crash.

2. By taking a brisk two-mile walk every day will help you live to be a hundred.

3. As for an example would be Nick Nolte, who has played a wide range of roles.

4. To assemble this container using ordinary household glue.

5. In New York, one of the world's most populated cities, has a broad sample of the human species.

CUMULATIVE EXERCISE ON CORRECTNESS

The following paragraphs contain errors. Make the necessary changes in spelling, verb or pronoun agreement, sentence correctness, and punctuation.

Antarctica is one of the most desolate places on earth, it's impossibly cold climate makes it uninhabitable. Scientist go their to study many animals. Such as the penguins, seabirds, whales, and seals. Scientists also study the icebergs, the atmosphere, and observe the stars. They even drill down into the icebergs and 5 remove long samples of ice, called ice cores so that they can study the air deep in the ice, signs of volcanic eruptions, and pollen grains that are thousands of years old. They also have found that fish are able to live way below sea level, down under the icebergs.

But noone lives there for to long. Everything, all food and supplies, 10 have to be flown in. The weather is brutal. Temperatures can drop to minus one hundred degrees Fahrenheit and winds can reach two hundred miles per hour. When the sun sinks below the horizon in the middle of March Antarctica is left in the dark for six mos. The only light comes from the moon, the stars and the southern lights 15 (Aurora Australis).

Introductions and Conclusions

1. After you've finished the exercise on "Finding an Organization for your Essay" (on p. 114)— or an essay that you've already written— use the following guidelines to write three introductions that you might use.

   - Start with a shocking statement

   - Start with an opinion you wish to oppose

   - Start with a brief story

2. Now write three conclusions, using these guidelines:

   - Sum up your main points

   - Raise further questions or implications

   - Put your ideas in a wider perspective

Paragraphs—Long and Short

Write a well-developed paragraph on one of the following topics. Be sure to give the specific details and to stick to *one main idea*. Before starting each topic, list a number of points you might use; then choose the best point and write your paragraph to back it up.

1. One strength or weakness that you have

2. One reason you chose your college

3. One statement summing up the style of the room you are in right now

4. One good point or one bad point about the president of the United States

Transitions

Choose one of the transition words from the following list to complete each sentence below. Be certain that the word you choose makes sense in the context of the sentence. Do not use the same word more than twice.

Consequently	therefore	furthermore	since
in fact	however	eventually	though
nevertheless	above all	for example	finally

Example: _Since_ the snake was creeping towards us, we.grabbed a pointed stick.

1. Sleep is necessary to good mental health; _____, too much sleep can sometimes lead to depression.

2. Someone who plays the piano, _____, can add a lot to a party.

3. If you're planning to become a social worker, _____, it's very important to get a master's degree.

4. _____, jasmine oil can also be used as an aid for relaxation.

5. I threatened to call the police. _____, the man gave me back my wallet.

6. _____ do not fail to sign your tax return or it will be

promptly returned to you.

7 ._____ UPS will not deliver to a post office box, I will mail

the package parcel post.

8. Mrs. Lacy avoids the sun completely; _____, she carries a

parasol whenever she goes out.

9. _____, France raised $400,000 in order to build the Statue

of Liberty as a gift to America.

10. Hard work usually pays off. _____, Steve Jobs and Steve

Wozniak created the Apple computer in their garage.

Writing Activity

Write a short essay— at least three paragraphs—
about going on a trip. Make a conscious effort to
use appropriate transitions both between
sentences and between paragraphs.

Proofreading

Proofread and correct the following paragraph for typographical and other errors. For example, the first line should be corrected to read:

Millions of people suffer from sleep disorders. Although

Milllions of people suffer from sleep disorders and, although sleep

disorders are not exactly dangerous to one's health, they are

excruciating for those who have them. Some times sleep disorders

can be alleviated by simple methods such as going ot bed later,

drinking less caffeine, or undertaking a mild exercise routine at   5

bedtime. Often, however,the problem doesn't go away so easily

and eventually people who suffer from prolonged sleep disorders

will develop other other health problems, such as constant fatigue,

depression, migraine headaches, and a general breafdown of the

immune system. But thats not all. Sleep disorders are expensive.   10

Sufferers have to pay for treatment out of there own pockets since

most insurance companies do not recognize sleep disorders a a

medical problem, however, since Sleep disorders are   not

regarded as a major health threat, little medical research is being

done on them and therefore no real treatments have been   15 developed. Until medical science, decides that sleep disorders are

a serious problem which must be addressed, millions of people will

continue to walk the floor night after night and suffer alone,   20

without hope.

Proofreading

Proofread and correct the following paragraphs for typographical and other errors.

For example, the first sentence should be corrected to read:

One of the most influential books of the past century is <u>Uncle Tom's Cabin</u>. Although

One of the most influential books of the past century is <u>Uncle

Tom's Cabin</u>. Although some critics consider it sentimental,

overwritten, and contrived, nearlrly everyone acknowledges that

the book did much to inst9gate the American civil War.

Harriet Beecher Stowe, the author the the book, grew up in a   5

home which often offered refuge to runaway slaves who were

escaping on the Underground Railroad into Canada. As a young

girl, Stowe heard many stores directly from the mouths of these

slaves about the horrors they had endured. Her feeelings for these

abused people, coupled with her religious fervor, inspired her to do   10

something to help such a help correct such a wrong.

Stowe's father, brothers, and husband were all ministers who

fought against slavery from the pulpit. When her sister-in law wrote

to her, pleading wih her to "write something that would make a whole nation feel what an accursed thing slavery is," Stowe   15

Resolved that she would do so. She wrote what she considered the

climax of the story—Tom's death—first and then went back and

wrote the beginnig of the story. In 18511, the <u>National Era</u>, an

antislavery paper, began serialization off the book and, when the

book itself was issued in 1852, it sold out within two days. Uncle   20

Tom's Cabin made Stowe an international figure, despised by some

and admired by most.. President Abraham Lincoln honored her and

called her the "lady who wrote the book that made this big war."

Proofreading

Proofread and correct the following paragraphs for typographical and other errors.

For example, the first line should be corrected to read:

If you ever drive through Mississippi, you might be surprised to

If you ever drive through Missippippi, you might be surprised to

see the diversity of landscape. HJeading into the state form

Memphis, Tennesseee, you'll pass Oxford, home of Ole Miss, and

within minutes you'll be driving up and down very thick forested

hills which are covered in kudzu, a rich gree climbing vine that is   5

indestructible.

Leaving the northern part of the state state, you will enter a

very low valley call the Delta—so named because of its similarity

to the delta rgion in Egypt. For many decades, the delta's rich

fertile soil produced outstanding cotten crops and put mississippi   10

on the map as the center of the cotton industry.

After you pass througfh the Delta region, you'll begin a climb again

and with in an hour will arrive at a small ciyt nestled into romantic

bluffs overlooking the Mississippi River. This is Vicksburg, the site

of one of the most decisive battles of the War between the States   15

At this point, you can travel along the Missssippi River down to

Natchez where still stand some of the most magnificient ante-

bellum mansions in the America. From Natchez you can go down

into St Francisville Louisiana, and stop to see several large old

plantations where sugar sane used to grown.   20

    However , if you want to take another see the rest of the state,

you can drive west from Vicksburg and in an hour you'll be in

Jackson, the state's capital, and the only city in Mississippi with a

population of over 150,000. From Jackson, you'l;l descend again

through the flat piney lumber region which takes you through   25

Hattiesburg and then on to the Gulf Coast. The coast, situaated

along a twenty-mile beach overlooking the Gulf of mexico, is dotted

with unusual little shrimping towns such as Biloxi, Ocean Springs,

and Bay St. Louis. From the coast, it's only a ninety-minute drive

along eth Gulf of Mexico to America's most exotic city—New   30

Orleans, "The City that Care Forgot"

Proofreading

Proofread and correct the following paragraph for typographical and other errors. For example, the first sentence should be corrected to read:

Every March the emperor penguins, found in Antarctica, gather together in huge masses on the bare ice.

Every march, the emperor penguins, found in Antarctica, gather

together in huge masses on the bare ice. The emperor is the

largest species of penguin. Their weight; is about 65 pounds and

they stand almost four feet tall. They dont build nests. The femal

lays a single large single large egg. She doesn't allow it to lie on the   5

bare ice,but passes it from her large webbed feet to the male's

feet. Then all the males huddle together with the eggs on their

feet. A loose fold of skin covers each egg and keeps it warm.

Whilethe males incubate the eggs in this strange manner, huddling

together for warmth in colonies of up to 5,000, the females head   10

off to sea to feed. The males stand there, braving the coldest

weather conditions on earth, with no food, for up to two months.

They survive on their body fat a lone. Two months later the females

return with full bellies; the eggs hatch and the males, weak and

hungry, with half their body weight gone, waddle to the sea for a   15

well-earned meal.

127

PART III

Meeting Specific Assignments

Format

The page below has numerous errors of format. See how many you can list.

"DREAMS"

by *Lee Dunsworth*

In the Old Testament, Joseph interpreted the dreams of Pharaoh and prophesied the future. Ever since, people have believed that dreams carry secret kno-wledge. For centuries they thought that through dreams they could learn the future. But in 1900, [5] Sigmund Freud turned dream interpretation on its head:he used dreams to understand the past. Most psychotherapists follow Freud's example. However ,some modern neuroanatomists question whether dreams mean anything at all. [10]

In the Bible, Joseph interpreted dreams on two occasions.

Writing in Class

Choose one of the following topics:

Evaluate someone who has supervised your work—currently or in the past. How well does this person do his or her job?

Compare your home to a home that you have visited which is very different from yours.

Now take fifteen minutes to do the following steps for the topic you have chosen:

1. List as many points as you can for use in an essay. Write a word or phrase for each.

2. Under each point, list examples that would demonstrate or support that point.

3. Decide on two or three main points and the examples or reasons that will make each point clear.

4. Plan the order of these points.

5. Write an introduction to the essay, indicating your main points.

Writing in Class

For practice in writing under pressure, set a timer for an hour and write an essay on one of the following topics. Plan for ten minutes; write for forty minutes; and proofread for ten minutes.

1. Recall an experience—good or bad—which changed your life. Describe the experience briefly and then explain in detail its influence on you.

2. Think of something you want in your life right now, and explain two or three reasons why you want it.

3. Argue one side or the other on the use of corporal punishment in the home.

How to Quote from Your Sources

Here is the "Postscript" from *Rules of Thumb*:

> You do your best work when you take pleasure in a job. You write best when you know something about the topic and know what you want to stress. So, when you can, write about a topic you've lived with and have considered over time. When you *have* to write about a topic that seems boring or difficult, get to know it for a while, until it makes sense to you. Start with what is clear to you and you will write well.
>
> Don't quit too soon. Sometimes a few more changes, a little extra attention to fine points, a new paragraph written on a separate piece of paper will transform an acceptable essay into an essay that really pleases you. Through the time you spend writing and rewriting, you will discover what is most important to say.

5

10

1. Write a summary of the "Postscript" in two sentences.

2. Use the authors' names (Silverman, Hughes, and Wienbroer) in a sentence and give a direct quotation from the "Postscript. "

3. Select a word or short phrase that you find important and write a sentence telling why. Include the word or phrase in your sentence.

4. Respond to the advice in the beginning of the second paragraph: "Don't quit too soon. " Write two or three sentences based on your own experience. Include the quotation within one of your sentences.

5. State an opinion about the "Postscript, " followed by a quotation from it that illustrates your point of view.

Using the College Library
and the Internet

Using the public access catalog or computerized catalog, find the answers to the following questions:

1. What is the very first book about the subject "music" listed in the catalog?

2. How many titles by Willa Cather are in your college library?

3. Write down the city of publication, the name of the publisher, and the date of publication of *Working*, by Studs Terkel.

4. Find the call number for *The Prairie Years*, by Carl Sandburg. Go to the stacks and find out whether it is on the shelf. Write down the titles of three books you find closest to its place on the shelf.

Find the answers to the following questions by using the library resources indicated:

5. Using an Internet search engine such as *Altavista* or *Yahoo*, find several articles about wolves in Yellowstone National Park.

6. How did Joe DiMaggio do at bat on 17 June 1941? Use *The New York Times* on microfilm or CD-ROM.

7. When, in 1863, did New Yorkers learn of the fall of Vicksburg, Mississippi, to Union forces? Use *The New York Times Index*.

8. What is the origin of the phrase "rule of thumb"? Consult the Oxford English Dictionary (OED).

9. How many articles about President John F. Kennedy were listed in *The Reader's Guide to Periodical Literature* for 1990?

10. On the Internet, go to www.dejanews.com and submit a query "Why are barns painted red?" Review the answers until you find the most plausible explanation.

137

Using the College Library and the Internet

Choose one of the following writers for a bibliographical search:

James Baldwin
Flannery O'Connor
Leo Tolstoy
Langston Hughes
Henrik Ibsen
Edith Wharton

1. Write down the years of the writer's birth and death.

2. Write down the titles, publishers, and original years of publication of three books by the writer.

3. Write down the authors, titles, and years of publication of three books about the writer.

4. Write down the authors, titles, names of periodicals, dates, and pages of three articles about the writer.

5. Use either the Humanities Citation Index or CARL.ORG to find an article on one of the authors.

Note: Internet information from Rules of Thumb is regularly updated on the McGraw-Hill Website at www.mhhe.com/writers

Writing Research Papers

Make believe that these are some of your notes from research on pizza. You were very careful when taking notes, so only the words surrounded by quotation marks are direct quotations; all other phrases are already paraphrased (in your own words), and you double-checked the page references before you left the library.

Notes

Jeff Smith advises adding just one extra ingredient to tomato sauce and cheese on the dough— for example, tomatoes, or onions, or potatoes "arranged like tiles. " He also says to "drizzle some good olive oil over the whole thing" before baking (487).

Alice Waters makes a pizza with a layer of tomatoes and a layer of shrimp sautéed with scallions; she adds chopped basil and parsley after baking. There is no cheese. She also says to "Try this pizza with a mixture of shellfish: squid tentacles, shrimp, mussels, scallops, and so on" (160).

In *The New York Times International Cookbook*, Craig Claiborne uses anchovy paste all over the dough before he spreads on the tomato sauce. Then he adds grated parmesan and chopped mozzarella. This is his basic recipe, but he omits the anchovy paste when he adds mushrooms or pepperoni (440).

1. First read over the notes to familiarize yourself with the information.

2. Next, put these notes aside and write a paragraph about your own favorite pizza combinations.

3. Now add information from your notes to your paragraph where it will fit in smoothly to support your remark or contrast with what you have

already written. Include at least two direct quotations.

4. Add transition words and phrases, such as *according to*, *on the other hand*, *in contrast*, or *similarly*.

5. Add parenthetical citations as needed.

6. Revise your paragraph for logical order, and edit for correctness.

Writing Research Papers

Consult a newspaper, watch television news, or listen to a public radio station (or an all-news network). Take notes on a major event that is reported—such as a sports game, a political announcement, a person's accomplishment, an unusual accident, or a weather story. Be sure to write down at least one phrase, word for word. If you are getting the story on radio or on television, you might want to tape-record the broadcast.

Now write a paragraph which summarizes the event, incorporating the quotation as well as your own comments. Make sure that most of the paragraph is in your own words. Be sure to acknowledge your source.

For example, you might begin:

Today the city council approved a new recycling law that will affect every citizen in our locality. The mayor announced, ". . .

Plagiarism

Here is a passage from page 22 of Jack London's account of the San Francisco earthquake of 1906:

> The earthquake shook down in San Francisco hundreds of thousands of dollars worth of walls and chimneys. But the conflagration that followed burned up hundreds of millions of dollars worth of property. There is no estimating within hundreds of millions the actual damage wrought.
> — "The Story of an Eyewitness." *Collier's Weekly* 5 May 1906: 22–23.

Which of the following statements in a term paper must give credit to Jack London in order to avoid plagiarism? Insert quotation marks where necessary.

1. The San Francisco earthquake of 1906 shook down hundreds of thousands of dollars worth of walls and chimneys. The conflagration that followed burned up hundreds of millions of dollars worth of property.

2. The earthquake of 1906 caused hundreds of millions of dollars in damage——both directly (by knocking down structures) and indirectly (by igniting fires) throughout San Francisco.

3. Earthquakes often destroy much of the property and wealth of a city.

4. One account of the San Francisco earthquake estimated that hundreds of millions of dollars in property was burned in fires caused by the earthquake.

5. The San Francisco earthquake of 1906 knocked down many buildings and virtually destroyed the city.

Documentation

PARENTHETICAL CITATION

Here is a sample paragraph from a research paper on pizza. Identify the places where parenthetical citations are needed—that is, where the information is not common knowledge—and mark them.

For example, a parenthetical citation is needed at the end of the first sentence:

> A *New Yorker* cartoon shows two technicians puzzling over a slice of pizza at "The Bureau of Unidentified Pizza Toppings" (   ).

A *New Yorker* cartoon shows two technicians puzzling over a slice of

pizza at "The Bureau of Unidentified Pizza Toppings." Pizza—with all

its various toppings—is one of the most popular food items in

America. In fact, Leonard Lopate reports that over 20,000 acres of

pizza are consumed daily in the United States. From childhood,   5

Americans eat pizza—at birthday parties, after school or sports

events, on their first dates, or while at work on projects. In

particular, pizza is a wise choice for a quick meal when there's a

work deadline: It doesn't require utensils. It's the lowest in calories

of the three most popular fast-food meals, and it is nutritionists' first   10

choice. Pizza is such standard fare during overtime that news

reporters regularly monitor Domino's Pizzas' deliveries to the White

House to see if a presidential announcement is forthcoming.

144

Documentation

PARENTHETICAL CITATION

Assume that you're writing a paper about Hoagy Carmichael and one of your sources is the following paragraph:

> "Star Dust," the most recorded song in the history of American music, was written in 1927 by Hoagy Carmichael, one of the most inventive composers of our day. Within a few years, the song made Carmichael a famous and wealthy man who then gave up a career as a lawyer to become a full-time musician. He went on to write many other classics—such as "Georgia," "The Nearness of You," and "I Get Along Without You Very Well"—but "Stardust" continued to be the most popular. According to Ronny Schiff, Carmichael got "letters from people the world over telling about romances that bloomed because of this song" (28).
> —"The Music of Hoagy Carmichael," by Elaine Hughes, p. 2.

1. Use the author's name in a sentence and give a direct quotation.

2. Write a sentence including a fact from the article.

3. Comment on a word or short phrase the author used.

4. Write a sentence that includes the quotation at the end of the paragraph.

5. Write a sentence that summarizes the main point of the paragraph.

Now add the appropriate parenthetical citation after each sentence. Make sure that the period at the end of each sentence is *after* the closing parenthesis of the citation.

Note: The quotation from Ronny Schiff comes from her book,

Hoagy Carmichael: The Stardust Melodies of. . . .
Melville, NY: Belwin, 1983.

The American people have an obsession with personal cleanliness; that is why the market for soaps, shampoos, and deodorants is such a good one. No matter what the marketing strategy, such products will always sell. It is not a coincidence that to be clean and well deodorized has become especially desirable since the invention of television. Surely, the last forty or fifty years have been particularly well deodorized because television tells us that being clean and smelling good is desirable.

However, long before television and the mass media, we were a rather dirty bunch of human beings. Today, we take for granted a simple shower or bath with soap and fresh clean water, but in the past keeping clean was not quite so simple. In fact, a clean and deodorized America would be shocked at how seldom our recent ancestors bathed. After all, people didn't always have deodorant and soap, so sometimes plain water had to suffice (plain water that was not clean in and of itself, to say the least). How did they do it? How did they keep clean in medieval times and

in the Victorian Age? They didn't do it very
well, and there is an enormous difference between   25
the personal habits of the rich and the poor back
in those times.

    Medieval England was a dangerous place to
live. Frances and Joseph Gies explain that often
the plague was rampant and the person who was   30
lucky enough to live past childhood usually did
not live past the age of forty-five (121).
Medieval peasants rarely if ever bathed, and one
can only wonder if the spread of the plague and
other diseases could have been curbed with the use   35
of a little personal hygiene. Gathering the water
was a great deal of work, so unless it was
specified for cooking, it was not seen as worth
the effort. Gies and Gies tell how a family of
five would take their baths about once a month and   40
usually use the same bath water in succession. A
barrel with the top removed served as a bathing
vessel (93). On a particularly dirty day, say, if
a peasant was covered in mud from working in the
fields, he or she might wash with some plain water   45
to get rid of the grime (Buehr 134). Farm animals
moved freely in and out of the hovels and slept a

150

matter of a few feet away from the occupants of

the home (Howarth 12). When tidying up the house

it was normal to sweep up animal dung along with **50**

the rest of the dirt on the floor (Gies and Gies

92-93). In towns, some people bathed in public

bath houses called "stews." Stews were well known

for having open nudity between the sexes, and

loose women could frequently be found there (Buehr **55**

134). No wonder there was so much death from

disease.

The rich lived slightly differently in

medieval times. Some of the rich saw baths as

having medicinal qualities. King John washed in **60**

"sweet green herbs" with "five or six sponges to

sit upon" and rinsed with rosewater (Hassall 210).

A contemporary record of these procedures explains

that first one would "boil leaves and herbs" and

then **65**

> Throw them hot into a vessel and put your
>
> lord over it and let him endure it for a
>
> while . . . whatever disease, grievance or
>
> pain ye be vexed with, this medicine will
>
> surely make you whole. . . . (qtd. in **70**
>
> Hassall 211)

151

Apparently the rich had the luxury of using baths
as a cure for ills while the poor used them
sparingly. Still, rich and poor of medieval times
were both afflicted with insects and vermin. It   75
was a rare person who wasn't tormented by lice and
fleas (Collis 10). One can only wonder if this
was because of the lack of real soap rather than
herbs & leaves. Charles Panati reports that soap
dates back to the Phoenicians in 600 BC, but soap   80
production "virtually came to a halt" in the
Middle Ages when the Christian Church forbade
"exposing the flesh, even to bathe" (218).

   I'm not sure what happened to "cleanliness is
next to godliness," but even before the Church   85
made modesty more important than getting rid of
dirt, it was clear that the English society didn't
care much for sanitation. The Romans had
introduced the concepts of sewage disposal and
providing a clean water supply for drinking and   90
bathing to England in 43 AD, but Quennell and
Quennell write that "Incredible as it may sound,
no real advance was made for 1400 years; from the
early fifth century until the beginning of the

nineteenth century people were not concerned with   95

Public Health" (88).

Things did not get much better--at least for
the poor--in Victorian England. Many people think
that the Victorians were prudish about their
bodies and therefore would not allow themselves to   100
go unwashed. This is only partially true. In
Victorian England the well-to-do were the ones who
kept stately homes and wore fine clothes. The
wealthy had frequent baths and washed daily with
water and soap (Childers 406). A basin was kept   105
in the bedroom and every morning it was filled
with fresh water to wash with. When the regular
bath was taken, a high-backed tub called a "hip
bath" was placed on the bedroom floor over some
towels to catch any water that splashed out. The   110
servants carried fresh hot water up in metal cans.
The whole process was laborious, but the
Victorians enjoyed it a great deal. At this point
there were bathrooms, but most wealthy Victorians
preferred to bathe in their rooms. The thought of   115
sharing bathing facilities with other family
members was repugnant to them (Quennell and
Quennell 71).

153

The poor were not so lucky in Victorian

England. Since the poorer class accounted for the **120**

masses in Victorian England, a great many people

lived in filth and muck. According to E. Royston

Pike, it was normal for two or three families to

live in one room (at a lodging house) and to

urinate and defecate in a pail in the center of **125**

the room. Beds were always filthy and full of

worms and insects; people were plagued by lice and

fleas (Pike 298-99). The rooms in the lodging

houses were usually unventilated and waterless.

In 1849, medical reports explained how leaking **130**

pipes released contaminated water into the London

reservoir; thus a whole neighborhood could be

contaminated by water containing raw sewage (qtd.

in Pike 306). The 1850 *London News* reported

"routine city flooding when the Thames 'backed up'" **135**

(qtd. in Gayman). Sometimes water lines would

run through cemeteries and pick up decomposing

animal matter (Pike 281). When the people did

bathe, either the water was black with dirt and

sewage or dripped sparingly from a pipe that a **140**

whole village waited in line to use (Pike 79).

Ironically, the lodging houses would not admit

154

people unless they had cleaned their feet (Pike 298).

It is entirely possible that the obsession with cleanliness that we know today stems from the modern knowledge that filth breeds disease. However, I think that this knowledge has evolved into neuroticism. It is not enough to be thin and beautiful or rich and handsome. One must be fresh and clean too. That brings to mind a commercial for a deodorant that I saw just recently. A young woman ruminates on how gross it is when she gets really close and a guy smells bad. I think this is why the producers of that deodorant make so much money; they shame us into buying their product. The poet Galway Kinnell calls advertisers "anti-prostitutes" because they "loathe human flesh for money" (43).

Still, when I walk into a store or a classroom and my nose is invaded by the stench of someone's body odor, I cannot help but wonder if he or she has seen that commercial or passed by the deodorant aisle of the supermarket lately. It occurs to me that television has gotten me too. Perhaps if I were back in Victorian or medieval times, I wouldn't care so much about that person's

body odor; but then again, neither of us would

have much choice.

Works Cited

Buehr, Walter. When Towns Had Walls: Life in a
Medieval English Town. New York: Crowell, 1970.

Childers, Joseph W. "Observation and
Representation: Mr. Chadwick Writes the Poor."
Victorian Studies 37 (1994) 405-31.

Collis, Louise. Memoirs of a Medieval Woman: The
Life and Times of Margery Kempe. New York:
Perennial, 1983.

Gayman, Mary. "The Badd Olde Days." Cleaner. n.d.
Cole Pub. [Three Lakes, WI]. 25 Oct. 1997
<http://klingon.util.utexas.edu/londonsewers/
londontext3.html>.

Gies, Frances, and Joseph Gies. Life in a Medieval
Village. New York: Harper, 1990.

Hassall, W. O. Medieval England as Viewed by
Contemporaries. New York: Harper, 1967.

Howarth, Sarah. Medieval Places. Brookfield, CT:
Millbrook, 1992.

Kinnell, Galway. "The Dead Shall Be Raised
Incorrectible." Book of Nightmares. Boston:
Houghton, 1971. 39-43.

Panati, Charles. Extraordinary Origins of Everyday
Things. New York: Harper, 1987.

Pike, E. Royston. Golden Times: Human Documents of

the Victorian Age. New York: Praeger, 1967.

Quennell, Marjorie, and C.H.B. Quennell. A History

of Everyday Things in England: The Rise of

Industrialism. London: B.T. Batsford, 1933.

PART IV

Writing
with
Elegance

Finding Your Voice

Here are some experiments to try, to help you discover the range of your writing voice. Write quickly, with energy; do each exercise for at least five minutes.

1. **Complain:** Get out your thoughts about something that bothers you.

2. **Curse:** Tell what you'd like to have happen to someone who makes you mad.

3. **Praise:** Tell how wonderful someone or something is.

4. **Teach:** In a helpful, encouraging way, tell a beginner how to do a simple task you do well.

5. **Be blunt:** Tell it like it is. Say the truth about something most people don't admit.

6. **Be sarcastic:** Throw scorn on something despicable.

Write a letter to someone important to you. Tell that person exactly what you couldn't say face-to-face, being as honest as you are able. You don't have to send the letter . . . but you might decide to do so.

Adding Details

Here are three general statements. Choose one and write a paragraph using details to illustrate it.

1. You can tell a lot about any family by looking at the inside and outside of the family's refrigerator.

2. Traveling on $20 a day can be a lot of fun.

3. When you're in physical pain, the world becomes a different place.

Write down every detail you can observe about each of the following items. When possible, describe what you can sense about the item using your eyes, ears, nose, fingers, and tongue. Take fifteen to twenty minutes for each, writing as you observe. When you think you have noticed everything, pause and then observe again.

1. An apple

2. The space you are in—a circle of a three-foot radius around you

3. A tree

4. A photograph from a magazine

5. An article of clothing

Recognizing Clichés

1. Make a list of clichés you hear at a social gathering or during one hour of television and rewrite them to make them fresh.

2. Describe a situation in which people use clichés. Tell what each person says and what you think is really going through the mind of one or all of the people involved. Write several pages if you can.

   Some possibilities:

   - a first date
   - being stopped by a police officer
   - consulting a doctor
   - seeing a former friend
   - visiting a sick relative
   - having Thanksgiving dinner

Eliminating Biased Language

Rewrite the following sentences to eliminate bias. For example, examine the following sentence:

The local underwear factory is hiring seamstresses and machine repairmen.

This sentence can be revised to read:

The local underwear factory is hiring **people to sew** and **people to repair machines.**

1. The automobile repairman should bring his own tools for the training seminar.

2. Attorneys, dentists, and doctors often keep photographs of their wives and children on their desks for clients to admire.

3. The breadwinner of the family should list his income on line 2; the housewife's income, if any, is listed on line 3.

4. The sorority girls did a workmanlike job on their float for the homecoming parade.

5. The policemen don't have too many details about the robbery; the gunman left no clues to his identity, and the victim is still in a coma.

6. John Smith is a noted white writer.

7. Volunteers manned the telephones during the fund drive.

8. This committee represents the entire community—all racial groups, a woman, and both religions.

9. The printing department is overworked: each teacher should have her copying requests submitted two weeks prior to the date needed.

10. Our airline provides top service: all repairmen use the latest aerotechnology, the stewardesses work solely for passenger safety and comfort, and the pilot is always the best in his class.

Trimming Wordiness

The following sentences can be condensed. Cross out excess words and rephrase if necessary. For example, examine the following sentence:

At six p.m. in the evening, the sound of church bells could be heard in the air.

This sentence can be trimmed to read:

At six in the evening, the church bells rang.

1. Lily Tomlin is a woman who has a zany and offbeat personality.

2. At that point in time, the officers proceeded to make an official arrest of the bank president.

3. John Kennedy was a person who enjoyed a good, humorous joke.

4. The reason why Vice-President Agnew left office was because of taking a bribe secretly.

5. In my opinion I think that Frank was not always pleasant to be around.

167

6. A slow drip could be noticed coming from the pipe under the sink in the kitchen.

7. Hot, spicy jalapeño chili peppers are something that Mexican chefs really love to use all the time.

8. Renata Bellini quit singing due to the fact that her audiences were not listening most of the time.

9. It really was so hot in Timbuktu during the month of January.

10. The bedspread's colorfast, engineered design provides refreshingly different, interesting, decorative accents for your bedroom.

Trimming Wordiness

In the following sentences, replace or delete most of the *being* verbs *(am, is, are, was, were, be, being, been).* You may have to rearrange the wording. For example, examine the following sentence:

> The basket of figs was left on the table by Mrs. Anchor, who is my cousin.

This sentence can be trimmed to read:

> Mrs. Anchor, my cousin, left the basket of figs on the table.

1. The rats were observed to be disoriented after the test substance was eaten by them.

2. Sophie is a grump who always makes life miserable for all of her friends; even when she is out of sight, the memory of her sour disposition is present.

3. The accident had been reported by the police, and within minutes the firetrucks were there.

4. The electronic percussion was added by the sound engineer after the keyboard solo had been recorded.

5. Our former suppliers have been changed because it was found that the contamination was caused by their negligence.

169

6. We were having a hard time loading the watermelons onto the truck because they were constantly rolling off and were breaking when they hit the concrete.

7. A man who was wearing a gray raincoat was being watched by the security officer because she suspected that he was shoplifting.

8. When life is tough, I am one of those people who are tougher.

9. In *The Kiss of the Spider Woman*, Sonia Braga's hair was long, her nails were long, and her skirt was tight; she was very glamorous.

10. It was sad to me when I was told that the old railroad depot was scheduled to be demolished.

Writing Activity

Write a paragraph relating an action you observed or took part in— for instance, a street fight, a roller coaster ride, or a dance. After you've written the paragraph, go back and circle all the *being* verbs (*am, is, are, was, were, be, being, been*). Then rewrite the paragraph eliminating all *being* verbs and replacing them with action verbs. In accomplishing the task, you may need to rewrite, combine, or eliminate some of your original sentences.

Varying Your Sentences

COMBINE CHOPPY SENTENCES

A good way to practice varying your sentences is by sentence-combining— taking five or six short sentences and reducing them to two or three. For example, examine the following group of short sentences:

1. Kevin started driving when he was only ten.

2. He drove a truck on his grandfather's farm in west Texas.

3. His grandfather could watch him on the farm roads.

4. He had the farm roads all to himself.

5. He learned to drive in a safe way.

Here are two ways that these sentences could be combined without losing any information:

> Kevin started driving a truck on his grandfather's farm in west Texas when he was only ten. Because he had the farm roads all to himself and his grandfather could keep an eye on him, he learned to drive in a safe way.

> When Kevin was only ten, he learned in safety to drive on his grandfather's farm in west Texas. Under his grandfather's eye, Kevin drove a truck on farm roads that he had to himself.

Varying Your Sentences

COMBINE CHOPPY SENTENCES

Combine the following sentences, retaining the facts. Each group should be reduced to two or three sentences. Be sure to use subordination or transition to show the relationship between the ideas. For an example, see p. 171.

1. The party was not a success.
2. The party ended in a major fight.
3. There was not enough food.
4. The hosts ran out of soda.
5. The guests hated the music.
6. The guest of honor left early.

1. They opened the menus.
2. They started looking at the vegetable dishes.
3. All of the people at the table were vegetarians.
4. They each ordered something different.
5. They decided to share.

Varying Your Sentences

COMBINE CHOPPY SENTENCES

Combine the following sentences, retaining the facts. Each group should be reduced to one or two sentences. Be sure to use subordination or transition to show the relationship between the ideas. For an example, see p. 171.

1. Bicycling in the city keeps you alert.

2. You have to concentrate on what is ahead of you.

3. You have to concentrate on what is behind you.

4. You have to concentrate on what is to either side of you.

5. Bicycling can be dangerous.

6. Bicycling also can be fun.

1. Marinate the chicken in a mixture of lemon, olive oil, and parsley.

2. Refrigerate the chicken in the mixture for two hours.

3. Grill it on a medium fire.

4. Brush it from time to time with the marinade.

5. Cook it for fifteen minutes.

6. Turn it over.

7. Cook it for fifteen minutes more.

Varying Your Sentences

COMBINE CHOPPY SENTENCES

Combine the following sentences, retaining the facts.
Each group should be reduced to one or two sentences.
Be sure to use subordination or transition to show the
relationship between the ideas. For an example, see p.
171.

1. He put the blank tape into the machine.
2. He rewound it.
3. The TV was on channel three.
4. The VCR was turned to "TV/VIDEO."
5. He pushed several buttons.
6. He unplugged the TV.
7. He went to the movies.

1. The platypus is a furry animal.
2. It lays eggs.
3. It has a bill like a duck.
4. It has a flat tail like a beaver.
5. It lives in and near water.
6. It has webbed feet.

Varying Your Sentences

STRONG ENDINGS

Rewrite the following sentences to give them stronger endings. For example, examine the parts of the following sentence:

Officer Langdon burned her uniform after witnessing the depth of the department's corruption.

The sentence can be made stronger by writing:

After witnessing the depth of the department's corruption, Officer Langdon burned her uniform.

1. Macon ended up with a broken leg when Evan's dog tripped him.

2. It poured for six days after two months of hot, dry weather, brown grass, and water rationing.

3. For the first time, she let him kiss her when the lights went out and the elevator got stuck between the fifth and sixth floors.

4. The state legislators were scandalized to learn about the retirement package—which totaled $900,000—of the school superintendent.

5. They sapped all the energy out of the writing in order to make the document politically correct.

6. The first volley of fireworks exploded in green and yellow showers as the crowd gazed towards the sky.

7. At last the mugger was arrested after attacking five people in one day and injuring two of them.

8. Nell Ann always comes through for us when the chips are down.

9. The audience cheered when one of the sisters threw flour on her face, jumped on the table, and danced a jig during the first act of *Dancing at Lughnasa*.

10. His hair was pulled back in a ponytail to reveal a new gold earring, which was the first thing that his mother noticed.

Varying Your Sentences

IMITATE GOOD WRITERS

Novels often begin with direct and memorable writing. Below you'll find the openings of four novels with a variety of styles. Use the structures of these sentences to write your own beginnings, matching your sentence rhythms to the author's but using your own subject matter.

For example, here is one imitation of Kafka's first sentence:

As she drove down the dirt road through the woods to her house that night, she noticed, hidden among the trees, a black pickup truck.

As Gregor Samsa awoke one morning from uneasy dreams, he found himself transformed in his bed into a gigantic insect.
— Franz Kafka, *The Metamorphosis*

I had the story, bit by bit, from various people, and, as generally happens in such cases, each time it was a different story.
— Edith Wharton, *Ethan Frome*

In that place, where they tore the nightshade and blackberry patches from their roots to make room for the Medallion City Golf Course, there was once a neighborhood. It stood in the hills above the valley town of Medallion and spread all the way to the river. It is called the suburbs now, but when black people lived there it was called the Bottom.
— Toni Morrison, *Sula*

From beyond the screen of bushes which surrounded the spring, Popeye watched the man drinking. A faint path led from the road to the spring. Popeye watched the man—a tall, thin man, hatless, in worn gray flannel trousers and carrying a tweed coat over his arm—emerge from the path and kneel to drink from the spring.
— William Faulkner, *Sanctuary*

177